BIRTH COMPASS: FIELDNOTES

Practice Makes Prepared

Birth Compass: Fieldnotes

Created by Samantha Vaive
Edited by Derek Vaive

This notebook is intended for personal use only.
It is designed as a supportive practice companion and is not a substitute for
medical care, mental health care, or individualized clinical guidance. Always
consult your care team for medical advice, diagnosis, or treatment.

Birth Compass and POGS are proprietary frameworks developed by Samantha
Vaive. Use of these materials for teaching, group facilitation, clinical programs,
or commercial purposes requires written permission.

First edition.

Lansing Michigan.

Welcome to Birth Compass: Fieldnotes

Fieldnotes are a place for interpretive insight, collecting data, and reflection. Here, you are the observer of your own experience. Awareness hones your skills for birth.

Practice makes prepared.

There are mark-making pages throughout this book. If you feel inclined, you can color, draw, doodle, write on them — or read the words and leave the pages as they are.

This is a place for you.
Low pressure. Low effort.
Still capable of shaping your birth experience.

There is no required way to use this notebook. Fill out every part every day. Skip days or sections. Use it however it fits into your life. This is a tool to support you, not a task you have to accomplish.

Enjoy the journey,
Dr. V

Day _____   **Date** _____

Today's Intention
circle one — or leave blank

Ground Soothe Rest Focus Release Curiosity Excitement

POGS Practice

PAUSE ☐
Take three intentional breaths.
Allow your breath shift your focus.

ORIENT ☐
Name three things you see _or_ three sensations you feel.
Allow your focus be specific.

GROUND ☐
Breathe intentionally, expanding your belly. Encourage your
exhales to be slightly longer than your inhales. Continue for 8
breaths. When you complete:
Allow your focus be on the feel of your body.

STEP ☐
Name one small adjustment that would support you right now.

_____

Body Check-In

Where do you feel tension?

_____

Where do you feel ease or neutrality?

_____

Field Note

Today I noticed...

_____

Preparation Note

If birth were happening today, what would help me most?

_____

Day _____   # Date _____

Today's Intention
circle one – or leave blank

Ground Soothe Rest Focus Release Curiosity Excitement

POGS Practice
PAUSE ☐
Take three intentional breaths.
Allow your breath shift your focus.

ORIENT ☐
Name three things you see *or* three sensations you feel.
Allow your focus be specific.

GROUND ☐
Breathe intentionally, expanding your belly. Encourage your
exhales to be slightly longer than your inhales. Continue for 8
breaths. When you complete:
Allow your focus be on the feel of your body.

STEP ☐
Name one small adjustment that would support you right now.

_____

Body Check-In

Where do you feel tension?

_____

Where do you feel ease or neutrality?

_____

Field Note

Today I noticed...

_____

Preparation Note

If birth were happening today, what would help me most?

_____

Day   Date

Today's Intention
circle one — or leave blank

Ground Soothe Rest Focus Release Curiosity Excitement

POGS Practice
PAUSE □
Take three intentional breaths.
Allow your breath shift your focus.

ORIENT □
Name three things you see or three sensations you feel.
Allow your focus be specific.

GROUND □
Breathe intentionally, expanding your belly. Encourage your
exhales to be slightly longer than your inhales. Continue for 8
breaths. When you complete:
Allow your focus be on the feel of your body.

STEP □
Name one small adjustment that would support you right now.

Body Check-In

Where do you feel tension?

Where do you feel ease or neutrality?

Field Note
Today I noticed...

Preparation Note
If birth were happening today, what would help me most?

Day

Date

Today's Intention
circle one — or leave blank

Ground   Soothe   Rest   Focus   Release   Curiosity   Excitement

POGS Practice

PAUSE ☐
Take three intentional breaths.
Allow your breath shift your focus.

ORIENT ☐
Name three things you see or three sensations you feel.
Allow your focus be specific.

GROUND ☐
Breathe intentionally, expanding your belly. Encourage your exhales to be slightly longer than your inhales. Continue for 8 breaths. When you complete:
Allow your focus be on the feel of your body.

STEP ☐
Name one small adjustment that would support you right now.

Body Check-In

Where do you feel tension?

Where do you feel ease or neutrality?

Field Note

Today I noticed...

Preparation Note

If birth were happening today, what would help me most?

Day _____   **Date** _____

Today's Intention
circle one – or leave blank

Ground   Soothe   Rest   Focus   Release   Curiosity   Excitement

POGS Practice
PAUSE ☐
Take three intentional breaths.
Allow your breath shift your focus.

ORIENT ☐
Name three things you see or three sensations you feel.
Allow your focus be specific.

GROUND ☐
Breathe intentionally, expanding your belly. Encourage your exhales to be slightly longer than your inhales. Continue for 8 breaths. When you complete:
Allow your focus be on the feel of your body.

STEP ☐
Name one small adjustment that would support you right now.

Body Check-In

Where do you feel tension?

Where do you feel ease or neutrality?

Field Note

Today I noticed...

Preparation Note

If birth were happening today, what would help me most?

Day _____   **Date** _____

Today's Intention
circle one — or leave blank

Ground   Soothe   Rest   Focus   Release   Curiosity   Excitement

POGS Practice

PAUSE ☐
Take three intentional breaths.
Allow your breath shift your focus.

ORIENT ☐
Name three things you see _or_ three sensations you feel.
Allow your focus be specific.

GROUND ☐
Breathe intentionally, expanding your belly. Encourage your exhales to be slightly longer than your inhales. Continue for 8 breaths. When you complete:
Allow your focus be on the feel of your body.

STEP ☐
Name one small adjustment that would support you right now.

_____

Body Check-In

Where do you feel tension?

_____

Where do you feel ease or neutrality?

_____

Field Note

Today I noticed...

_____

Preparation Note

If birth were happening today, what would help me most?

_____

Day _____   **Date** _____

Today's Intention
circle one — or leave blank

Ground   Soothe   Rest   Focus   Release   Curiosity   Excitement

POGS Practice

PAUSE ☐
Take three intentional breaths.
Allow your breath shift your focus.

ORIENT ☐
Name three things you see _or_ three sensations you feel.
Allow your focus be specific.

GROUND ☐
Breathe intentionally, expanding your belly. Encourage your exhales to be slightly longer than your inhales. Continue for 8 breaths. When you complete:
Allow your focus be on the feel of your body.

STEP ☐
Name one small adjustment that would support you right now.

Body Check-In

Where do you feel tension?

Where do you feel ease or neutrality?

Field Note

Today I noticed...

Preparation Note

If birth were happening today, what would help me most?

The Chaos Moves Around You But You Are Not the Chaos.

Day _____   **Date** _____

Today's Intention
circle one — or leave blank

Ground   Soothe   Rest   Focus   Release   Curiosity   Excitement

POGS Practice

PAUSE ☐
Take three intentional breaths.
Allow your breath shift your focus.

ORIENT ☐
Name three things you see _or_ three sensations you feel.
Allow your focus be specific.

GROUND ☐
Breathe intentionally, expanding your belly. Encourage your exhales to be slightly longer than your inhales. Continue for 8 breaths. When you complete:
Allow your focus be on the feel of your body.

STEP ☐
Name one small adjustment that would support you right now.

Body Check-In

Where do you feel tension?

Where do you feel ease or neutrality?

Field Note

Today I noticed...

Preparation Note

If birth were happening today, what would help me most?

Day _____   **Date** _____

Today's Intention
circle one — or leave blank

Ground   Soothe   Rest   Focus   Release   Curiosity   Excitement

POGS Practice

PAUSE ☐
Take three intentional breaths.
Allow your breath shift your focus.

ORIENT ☐
Name three things you see _or_ three sensations you feel.
Allow your focus be specific.

GROUND ☐
Breathe intentionally, expanding your belly. Encourage your exhales to be slightly longer than your inhales. Continue for 8 breaths. When you complete:
Allow your focus be on the feel of your body.

STEP ☐
Name one small adjustment that would support you right now.

_____

Body Check-In

Where do you feel tension?

_____

Where do you feel ease or neutrality?

_____

Field Note

Today I noticed...

_____

Preparation Note

If birth were happening today, what would help me most?

_____

Day _____   **Date** _____

Today's Intention
circle one – or leave blank

Ground   Soothe   Rest   Focus   Release   Curiosity   Excitement

POGS Practice
PAUSE ☐
Take three intentional breaths.
Allow your breath shift your focus.

ORIENT ☐
Name three things you see *or* three sensations you feel.
Allow your focus be specific.

GROUND ☐
Breathe intentionally, expanding your belly. Encourage your exhales to be slightly longer than your inhales. Continue for 8 breaths. When you complete:
Allow your focus be on the feel of your body.

STEP ☐
Name one small adjustment that would support you right now.

_____

Body Check-In

Where do you feel tension?

_____

Where do you feel ease or neutrality?

_____

Field Note

Today I noticed...

_____

Preparation Note

If birth were happening today, what would help me most?

_____

Day _____   **Date** _____

Today's Intention
circle one — or leave blank

Ground   Soothe   Rest   Focus   Release   Curiosity   Excitement

POGS Practice

PAUSE □
Take three intentional breaths.
Allow your breath shift your focus.

ORIENT □
Name three things you see *or* three sensations you feel.
Allow your focus be specific.

GROUND □
Breathe intentionally, expanding your belly. Encourage your
exhales to be slightly longer than your inhales. Continue for 8
breaths. When you complete:
Allow your focus be on the feel of your body.

STEP □
Name one small adjustment that would support you right now.

_____

Body Check-In

Where do you feel tension?

_____

Where do you feel ease or neutrality?

_____

Field Note

Today I noticed...

_____

Preparation Note

If birth were happening today, what would help me most?

_____

Day _____   **Date** _____

Today's Intention
circle one – or leave blank

Ground   Soothe   Rest   Focus   Release   Curiosity   Excitement

POGS Practice
PAUSE □
Take three intentional breaths.
Allow your breath shift your focus.

ORIENT □
Name three things you see *or* three sensations you feel.
Allow your focus be specific.

GROUND □
Breathe intentionally, expanding your belly. Encourage your
exhales to be slightly longer than your inhales. Continue for 8
breaths. When you complete:
Allow your focus be on the feel of your body.

STEP □
Name one small adjustment that would support you right now.

_____

Body Check-In

Where do you feel tension?

_____

Where do you feel ease or neutrality?

_____

Field Note

Today I noticed...

_____

Preparation Note

If birth were happening today, what would help me most?

_____

Day _____   **Date** _____

Today's Intention
circle one — or leave blank

Ground   Soothe   Rest   Focus   Release   Curiosity   Excitement

POGS Practice

PAUSE ☐
Take three intentional breaths.
Allow your breath shift your focus.

ORIENT ☐
Name three things you see *or* three sensations you feel.
Allow your focus be specific.

GROUND ☐
Breathe intentionally, expanding your belly. Encourage your
exhales to be slightly longer than your inhales. Continue for 8
breaths. When you complete:
Allow your focus be on the feel of your body.

STEP ☐
Name one small adjustment that would support you right now.

Body Check-In

Where do you feel tension?

Where do you feel ease or neutrality?

Field Note

Today I noticed...

Preparation Note

If birth were happening today, what would help me most?

Day

Date

Today's Intention
circle one — or leave blank

Ground   Soothe   Rest   Focus   Release   Curiosity   Excitement

POGS Practice
PAUSE □
Take three intentional breaths.
Allow your breath shift your focus.

ORIENT □
Name three things you see *or* three sensations you feel.
Allow your focus be specific.

GROUND □
Breathe intentionally, expanding your belly. Encourage your
exhales to be slightly longer than your inhales. Continue for 8
breaths. When you complete:
Allow your focus be on the feel of your body.

STEP □
Name one small adjustment that would support you right now.

Body Check-In

Where do you feel tension?

Where do you feel ease or neutrality?

Field Note

Today I noticed...

Preparation Note

If birth were happening today, what would help me most?

Freezing is inaction.
Pausing is intentional.

Day _____   **Date** _____

Today's Intention
circle one — or leave blank

Ground   Soothe   Rest   Focus   Release   Curiosity   Excitement

POGS Practice

PAUSE ☐
Take three intentional breaths.
Allow your breath shift your focus.

ORIENT ☐
Name three things you see *or* three sensations you feel.
Allow your focus be specific.

GROUND ☐
Breathe intentionally, expanding your belly. Encourage your
exhales to be slightly longer than your inhales. Continue for 8
breaths. When you complete:
Allow your focus be on the feel of your body.

STEP ☐
Name one small adjustment that would support you right now.

_____

Body Check-In

Where do you feel tension?

_____

Where do you feel ease or neutrality?

_____

Field Note

Today I noticed...

_____

Preparation Note

If birth were happening today, what would help me most?

_____

Day _____   **Date** _____

Today's Intention
circle one — or leave blank

Ground   Soothe   Rest   Focus   Release   Curiosity   Excitement

POGS Practice

PAUSE ☐
Take three intentional breaths.
Allow your breath shift your focus.

ORIENT ☐
Name three things you see *or* three sensations you feel.
Allow your focus be specific.

GROUND ☐
Breathe intentionally, expanding your belly. Encourage your exhales to be slightly longer than your inhales. Continue for 8 breaths. When you complete:
Allow your focus be on the feel of your body.

STEP ☐
Name one small adjustment that would support you right now.

_____

Body Check-In

Where do you feel tension?

_____

Where do you feel ease or neutrality?

_____

Field Note

Today I noticed...

_____

Preparation Note

If birth were happening today, what would help me most?

_____

Day _____ **Date** _____

Today's Intention
circle one — or leave blank

Ground   Soothe   Rest   Focus   Release   Curiosity   Excitement

POGS Practice

PAUSE ☐
Take three intentional breaths.
Allow your breath shift your focus.

ORIENT ☐
Name three things you see *or* three sensations you feel.
Allow your focus be specific.

GROUND ☐
Breathe intentionally, expanding your belly. Encourage your exhales to be slightly longer than your inhales. Continue for 8 breaths. When you complete:
Allow your focus be on the feel of your body.

STEP ☐
Name one small adjustment that would support you right now.

_____

Body Check-In

Where do you feel tension?

_____

Where do you feel ease or neutrality?

_____

Field Note

Today I noticed...

_____

Preparation Note

If birth were happening today, what would help me most?

_____

Day _____   **Date** _____

Today's Intention
circle one — or leave blank

Ground   Soothe   Rest   Focus   Release   Curiosity   Excitement

POGS Practice

PAUSE ☐
Take three intentional breaths.
Allow your breath shift your focus.

ORIENT ☐
Name three things you see *or* three sensations you feel.
Allow your focus be specific.

GROUND ☐
Breathe intentionally, expanding your belly. Encourage your
exhales to be slightly longer than your inhales. Continue for 8
breaths. When you complete:
Allow your focus be on the feel of your body.

STEP ☐
Name one small adjustment that would support you right now.

_____

Body Check-In

Where do you feel tension?

_____

Where do you feel ease or neutrality?

_____

Field Note

Today I noticed...

_____

Preparation Note

If birth were happening today, what would help me most?

_____

Day

Date

Today's Intention
circle one – or leave blank

Ground   Soothe   Rest   Focus   Release   Curiosity   Excitement

POGS Practice
PAUSE ☐
Take three intentional breaths.
Allow your breath shift your focus.

ORIENT ☐
Name three things you see *or* three sensations you feel.
Allow your focus be specific.

GROUND ☐
Breathe intentionally, expanding your belly. Encourage your exhales to be slightly longer than your inhales. Continue for 8 breaths. When you complete:
Allow your focus be on the feel of your body.

STEP ☐
Name one small adjustment that would support you right now.

Body Check-In

Where do you feel tension?

Where do you feel ease or neutrality?

Field Note

Today I noticed...

Preparation Note

If birth were happening today, what would help me most?

Day _____   # Date _____

Today's Intention
circle one — or leave blank

Ground   Soothe   Rest   Focus   Release   Curiosity   Excitement

POGS Practice

PAUSE ☐
Take three intentional breaths.
Allow your breath shift your focus.

ORIENT ☐
Name three things you see *or* three sensations you feel.
Allow your focus be specific.

GROUND ☐
Breathe intentionally, expanding your belly. Encourage your exhales to be slightly longer than your inhales. Continue for 8 breaths. When you complete:
Allow your focus be on the feel of your body.

STEP ☐
Name one small adjustment that would support you right now.

Body Check-In

Where do you feel tension?

Where do you feel ease or neutrality?

Field Note

Today I noticed...

Preparation Note

If birth were happening today, what would help me most?

Day _____   **Date** _____

Today's Intention
circle one — or leave blank

Ground   Soothe   Rest   Focus   Release   Curiosity   Excitement

POGS Practice

PAUSE ☐
Take three intentional breaths.
Allow your breath shift your focus.

ORIENT ☐
Name three things you see *or* three sensations you feel.
Allow your focus be specific.

GROUND ☐
Breathe intentionally, expanding your belly. Encourage your
exhales to be slightly longer than your inhales. Continue for 8
breaths. When you complete:
Allow your focus be on the feel of your body.

STEP ☐
Name one small adjustment that would support you right now.

Body Check-In

Where do you feel tension?

Where do you feel ease or neutrality?

Field Note

Today I noticed...

Preparation Note

If birth were happening today, what would help me most?

Let your thoughts
wander.
Let your hand
lead the way.

Day _____   **Date** _____

Today's Intention
circle one — or leave blank

Ground Soothe Rest Focus Release Curiosity Excitement

POGS Practice

PAUSE ☐
Take three intentional breaths.
Allow your breath shift your focus.

ORIENT ☐
Name three things you see _or_ three sensations you feel.
Allow your focus be specific.

GROUND ☐
Breathe intentionally, expanding your belly. Encourage your
exhales to be slightly longer than your inhales. Continue for 8
breaths. When you complete:
Allow your focus be on the feel of your body.

STEP ☐
Name one small adjustment that would support you right now.

Body Check-In

Where do you feel tension?

Where do you feel ease or neutrality?

Field Note

Today I noticed...

Preparation Note

If birth were happening today, what would help me most?

Day _____   **Date** _____

Today's Intention
circle one — or leave blank

Ground Soothe Rest Focus Release Curiosity Excitement

POGS Practice

PAUSE □
Take three intentional breaths.
Allow your breath shift your focus.

ORIENT □
Name three things you see _or_ three sensations you feel.
Allow your focus be specific.

GROUND □
Breathe intentionally, expanding your belly. Encourage your
exhales to be slightly longer than your inhales. Continue for 8
breaths. When you complete:
Allow your focus be on the feel of your body.

STEP □
Name one small adjustment that would support you right now.

_____

Body Check-In

Where do you feel tension?

Where do you feel ease or neutrality?

Field Note

Today I noticed...

Preparation Note

If birth were happening today, what would help me most?

Day _____   **Date** _____

Today's Intention
circle one — or leave blank

Ground Soothe Rest Focus Release Curiosity Excitement

POGS Practice
PAUSE □
Take three intentional breaths.
Allow your breath shift your focus.

ORIENT □
Name three things you see *or* three sensations you feel.
Allow your focus be specific.

GROUND □
Breathe intentionally, expanding your belly. Encourage your exhales to be slightly longer than your inhales. Continue for 8 breaths. When you complete:
Allow your focus be on the feel of your body.

STEP □
Name one small adjustment that would support you right now.

Body Check-In

Where do you feel tension?

Where do you feel ease or neutrality?

Field Note

Today I noticed...

Preparation Note

If birth were happening today, what would help me most?

Day _____   **Date** _____

Today's Intention
circle one — or leave blank

Ground   Soothe   Rest   Focus   Release   Curiosity   Excitement

POGS Practice

PAUSE ☐
Take three intentional breaths.
Allow your breath shift your focus.

ORIENT ☐
Name three things you see *or* three sensations you feel.
Allow your focus be specific.

GROUND ☐
Breathe intentionally, expanding your belly. Encourage your exhales to be slightly longer than your inhales. Continue for 8 breaths. When you complete:
Allow your focus be on the feel of your body.

STEP ☐
Name one small adjustment that would support you right now.

_____

Body Check-In

Where do you feel tension?

_____

Where do you feel ease or neutrality?

_____

Field Note

Today I noticed...

_____

Preparation Note

If birth were happening today, what would help me most?

_____

Day _____   **Date** _____

Today's Intention
circle one — or leave blank

Ground   Soothe   Rest   Focus   Release   Curiosity   Excitement

POGS Practice

PAUSE □
Take three intentional breaths.
Allow your breath shift your focus.

ORIENT □
Name three things you see _or_ three sensations you feel.
Allow your focus be specific.

GROUND □
Breathe intentionally, expanding your belly. Encourage your exhales to be slightly longer than your inhales. Continue for 8 breaths. When you complete:
Allow your focus be on the feel of your body.

STEP □
Name one small adjustment that would support you right now.

_____

Body Check-In

Where do you feel tension?

_____

Where do you feel ease or neutrality?

_____

Field Note

Today I noticed...

_____

Preparation Note

If birth were happening today, what would help me most?

_____

Day _____   **Date** _____

Today's Intention
circle one — or leave blank

Ground   Soothe   Rest   Focus   Release Curiosity Excitement

POGS Practice

PAUSE ☐
Take three intentional breaths.
Allow your breath shift your focus.

ORIENT ☐
Name three things you see *or* three sensations you feel.
Allow your focus be specific.

GROUND ☐
Breathe intentionally, expanding your belly. Encourage your
exhales to be slightly longer than your inhales. Continue for 8
breaths. When you complete:
Allow your focus be on the feel of your body.

STEP ☐
Name one small adjustment that would support you right now.

_____

Body Check-In

Where do you feel tension?

_____

Where do you feel ease or neutrality?

_____

Field Note

Today I noticed...

_____

Preparation Note

If birth were happening today, what would help me most?

_____

Day

Date

Today's Intention
circle one — or leave blank

Ground Soothe Rest Focus Release Curiosity Excitement

POGS Practice

PAUSE □
Take three intentional breaths.
Allow your breath shift your focus.

ORIENT □
Name three things you see *or* three sensations you feel.
Allow your focus be specific.

GROUND □
Breathe intentionally, expanding your belly. Encourage your exhales to be slightly longer than your inhales. Continue for 8 breaths. When you complete:
Allow your focus be on the feel of your body.

STEP □
Name one small adjustment that would support you right now.

Body Check-In

Where do you feel tension?

Where do you feel ease or neutrality?

Field Note

Today I noticed...

Preparation Note

If birth were happening today, what would help me most?

What do you need to let out?

Day _____   **Date** _____

Today's Intention
circle one — or leave blank

Ground   Soothe   Rest   Focus   Release   Curiosity   Excitement

POGS Practice

PAUSE ☐
Take three intentional breaths.
Allow your breath shift your focus.

ORIENT ☐
Name three things you see *or* three sensations you feel.
Allow your focus be specific.

GROUND ☐
Breathe intentionally, expanding your belly. Encourage your
exhales to be slightly longer than your inhales. Continue for 8
breaths. When you complete:
Allow your focus be on the feel of your body.

STEP ☐
Name one small adjustment that would support you right now.

_____

Body Check-In

Where do you feel tension?

_____

Where do you feel ease or neutrality?

_____

Field Note

Today I noticed...

_____

Preparation Note

If birth were happening today, what would help me most?

_____

Day _____   **Date** _____

Today's Intention
circle one — or leave blank

Ground   Soothe   Rest   Focus   Release   Curiosity   Excitement

POGS Practice

PAUSE ☐
Take three intentional breaths.
Allow your breath shift your focus.

ORIENT ☐
Name three things you see _or_ three sensations you feel.
Allow your focus be specific.

GROUND ☐
Breathe intentionally, expanding your belly. Encourage your
exhales to be slightly longer than your inhales. Continue for 8
breaths. When you complete:
Allow your focus be on the feel of your body.

STEP ☐
Name one small adjustment that would support you right now.

_____

Body Check-In

Where do you feel tension?

_____

Where do you feel ease or neutrality?

_____

Field Note

Today I noticed...

_____

Preparation Note

If birth were happening today, what would help me most?

_____

Day

Date

Today's Intention
circle one — or leave blank

Ground Soothe Rest Focus Release Curiosity Excitement

POGS Practice
PAUSE ☐
Take three intentional breaths.
Allow your breath shift your focus.

ORIENT ☐
Name three things you see *or* three sensations you feel.
Allow your focus be specific.

GROUND ☐
Breathe intentionally, expanding your belly. Encourage your
exhales to be slightly longer than your inhales. Continue for 8
breaths. When you complete:
Allow your focus be on the feel of your body.

STEP ☐
Name one small adjustment that would support you right now.

Body Check-In

Where do you feel tension?

Where do you feel ease or neutrality?

Field Note
Today I noticed...

Preparation Note
If birth were happening today, what would help me most?

Day _____   **Date** _____

Today's Intention
circle one — or leave blank

Ground   Soothe   Rest   Focus   Release Curiosity Excitement

POGS Practice

PAUSE ☐
Take three intentional breaths.
Allow your breath shift your focus.

ORIENT ☐
Name three things you see _or_ three sensations you feel.
Allow your focus be specific.

GROUND ☐
Breathe intentionally, expanding your belly. Encourage your
exhales to be slightly longer than your inhales. Continue for 8
breaths. When you complete:
Allow your focus be on the feel of your body.

STEP ☐
Name one small adjustment that would support you right now.

_____

Body Check-In

Where do you feel tension?

_____

Where do you feel ease or neutrality?

_____

Field Note

Today I noticed...

_____

Preparation Note

If birth were happening today, what would help me most?

_____

Today's Intention
circle one — or leave blank

Ground   Soothe   Rest   Focus   Release   Curiosity   Excitement

POGS Practice
PAUSE ☐
Take three intentional breaths.
Allow your breath shift your focus.

ORIENT ☐
Name three things you see *or* three sensations you feel.
Allow your focus be specific.

GROUND ☐
Breathe intentionally, expanding your belly. Encourage your
exhales to be slightly longer than your inhales. Continue for 8
breaths. When you complete:
Allow your focus be on the feel of your body.

STEP ☐
Name one small adjustment that would support you right now.

_____

Body Check-In

Where do you feel tension?

_____

Where do you feel ease or neutrality?

_____

Field Note

Today I noticed...

_____

Preparation Note

If birth were happening today, what would help me most?

_____

Day _____   **Date** _____

Today's Intention
circle one — or leave blank

Ground   Soothe   Rest   Focus   Release   Curiosity   Excitement

POGS Practice

PAUSE ☐
Take three intentional breaths.
Allow your breath shift your focus.

ORIENT ☐
Name three things you see or three sensations you feel.
Allow your focus be specific.

GROUND ☐
Breathe intentionally, expanding your belly. Encourage your exhales to be slightly longer than your inhales. Continue for 8 breaths. When you complete:
Allow your focus be on the feel of your body.

STEP ☐
Name one small adjustment that would support you right now.

_____

Body Check-In

Where do you feel tension?

_____

Where do you feel ease or neutrality?

_____

Field Note

Today I noticed...

_____

Preparation Note

If birth were happening today, what would help me most?

_____

Day _____   **Date** _____

Today's Intention
circle one — or leave blank

Ground   Soothe   Rest   Focus   Release   Curiosity   Excitement

POGS Practice

PAUSE □
Take three intentional breaths.
Allow your breath shift your focus.

ORIENT □
Name three things you see *or* three sensations you feel.
Allow your focus be specific.

GROUND □
Breathe intentionally, expanding your belly. Encourage your
exhales to be slightly longer than your inhales. Continue for 8
breaths. When you complete:
Allow your focus be on the feel of your body.

STEP □
Name one small adjustment that would support you right now.

_____

Body Check-In

Where do you feel tension?

_____

Where do you feel ease or neutrality?

_____

Field Note

Today I noticed...

_____

Preparation Note

If birth were happening today, what would help me most?

_____

It's okay to change
your mind
when things change.

Day _____   **Date** _____

Today's Intention
circle one — or leave blank

Ground   Soothe   Rest   Focus   Release   Curiosity   Excitement

POGS Practice

PAUSE □
Take three intentional breaths.
Allow your breath shift your focus.

ORIENT □
Name three things you see *or* three sensations you feel.
Allow your focus be specific.

GROUND □
Breathe intentionally, expanding your belly. Encourage your exhales to be slightly longer than your inhales. Continue for 8 breaths. When you complete:
Allow your focus be on the feel of your body.

STEP □
Name one small adjustment that would support you right now.

Body Check-In

Where do you feel tension?

Where do you feel ease or neutrality?

Field Note

Today I noticed...

Preparation Note

If birth were happening today, what would help me most?

Day

Date

Today's Intention
circle one — or leave blank

Ground   Soothe   Rest   Focus   Release   Curiosity   Excitement

POGS Practice

PAUSE ☐
Take three intentional breaths.
Allow your breath shift your focus.

ORIENT ☐
Name three things you see *or* three sensations you feel.
Allow your focus be specific.

GROUND ☐
Breathe intentionally, expanding your belly. Encourage your
exhales to be slightly longer than your inhales. Continue for 8
breaths. When you complete:
Allow your focus be on the feel of your body.

STEP ☐
Name one small adjustment that would support you right now.

Body Check-In

Where do you feel tension?

Where do you feel ease or neutrality?

Field Note

Today I noticed...

Preparation Note

If birth were happening today, what would help me most?

Day

Date

Today's Intention
circle one — or leave blank

Ground Soothe Rest Focus Release Curiosity Excitement

POGS Practice
PAUSE □
Take three intentional breaths.
Allow your breath shift your focus.

ORIENT □
Name three things you see *or* three sensations you feel.
Allow your focus be specific.

GROUND □
Breathe intentionally, expanding your belly. Encourage your
exhales to be slightly longer than your inhales. Continue for 8
breaths. When you complete:
Allow your focus be on the feel of your body.

STEP □
Name one small adjustment that would support you right now.

Body Check-In

Where do you feel tension?

Where do you feel ease or neutrality?

Field Note

Today I noticed...

Preparation Note

If birth were happening today, what would help me most?

Day _____   **Date** _____

Today's Intention
circle one — or leave blank

Ground   Soothe   Rest   Focus   Release   Curiosity   Excitement

POGS Practice

PAUSE ☐
Take three intentional breaths.
Allow your breath shift your focus.

ORIENT ☐
Name three things you see or three sensations you feel.
Allow your focus be specific.

GROUND ☐
Breathe intentionally, expanding your belly. Encourage your exhales to be slightly longer than your inhales. Continue for 8 breaths. When you complete:
Allow your focus be on the feel of your body.

STEP ☐
Name one small adjustment that would support you right now.

_____

Body Check-In

Where do you feel tension?

_____

Where do you feel ease or neutrality?

_____

Field Note

Today I noticed...

_____

Preparation Note

If birth were happening today, what would help me most?

_____

Day

Date

Today's Intention
circle one — or leave blank

Ground   Soothe   Rest   Focus   Release   Curiosity   Excitement

POGS Practice
PAUSE ☐
Take three intentional breaths.
Allow your breath shift your focus.

ORIENT ☐
Name three things you see *or* three sensations you feel.
Allow your focus be specific.

GROUND ☐
Breathe intentionally, expanding your belly. Encourage your
exhales to be slightly longer than your inhales. Continue for 8
breaths. When you complete:
Allow your focus be on the feel of your body.

STEP ☐
Name one small adjustment that would support you right now.

Body Check-In

Where do you feel tension?

Where do you feel ease or neutrality?

Field Note

Today I noticed...

Preparation Note

If birth were happening today, what would help me most?

Day _____   **Date** _____

Today's Intention
circle one — or leave blank

Ground   Soothe   Rest   Focus   Release   Curiosity   Excitement

POGS Practice

PAUSE □
Take three intentional breaths.
Allow your breath shift your focus.

ORIENT □
Name three things you see _or_ three sensations you feel.
Allow your focus be specific.

GROUND □
Breathe intentionally, expanding your belly. Encourage your
exhales to be slightly longer than your inhales. Continue for 8
breaths. When you complete:
Allow your focus be on the feel of your body.

STEP □
Name one small adjustment that would support you right now.

_____

Body Check-In

Where do you feel tension?

_____

Where do you feel ease or neutrality?

_____

Field Note

Today I noticed...

_____

Preparation Note

If birth were happening today, what would help me most?

_____

Day _____   # Date _____

Today's Intention
circle one — or leave blank

Ground   Soothe   Rest   Focus   Release   Curiosity   Excitement

POGS Practice

PAUSE ☐
Take three intentional breaths.
Allow your breath shift your focus.

ORIENT ☐
Name three things you see *or* three sensations you feel.
Allow your focus be specific.

GROUND ☐
Breathe intentionally, expanding your belly. Encourage your
exhales to be slightly longer than your inhales. Continue for 8
breaths. When you complete:
Allow your focus be on the feel of your body.

STEP ☐
Name one small adjustment that would support you right now.

Body Check-In

Where do you feel tension?

Where do you feel ease or neutrality?

Field Note

Today I noticed...

Preparation Note

If birth were happening today, what would help me most?

This Space is Yours

Day   **Date**

Today's Intention
circle one — or leave blank

Ground   Soothe   Rest   Focus   Release   Curiosity   Excitement

POGS Practice
PAUSE ☐
Take three intentional breaths.
Allow your breath shift your focus.

ORIENT ☐
Name three things you see *or* three sensations you feel.
Allow your focus be specific.

GROUND ☐
Breathe intentionally, expanding your belly. Encourage your
exhales to be slightly longer than your inhales. Continue for 8
breaths. When you complete:
Allow your focus be on the feel of your body.

STEP ☐
Name one small adjustment that would support you right now.

Body Check-In

Where do you feel tension?

Where do you feel ease or neutrality?

Field Note

Today I noticed...

Preparation Note

If birth were happening today, what would help me most?

Day _____   **Date** _____

Today's Intention
circle one — or leave blank

Ground   Soothe   Rest   Focus   Release   Curiosity   Excitement

POGS Practice

PAUSE □
Take three intentional breaths.
Allow your breath shift your focus.

ORIENT □
Name three things you see or three sensations you feel.
Allow your focus be specific.

GROUND □
Breathe intentionally, expanding your belly. Encourage your
exhales to be slightly longer than your inhales. Continue for 8
breaths. When you complete:
Allow your focus be on the feel of your body.

STEP □
Name one small adjustment that would support you right now.

Body Check-In

Where do you feel tension?

Where do you feel ease or neutrality?

Field Note

Today I noticed...

Preparation Note

If birth were happening today, what would help me most?

Day _____   **Date** _____

Today's Intention
circle one – or leave blank

Ground   Soothe   Rest   Focus   Release   Curiosity   Excitement

POGS Practice

PAUSE ☐
Take three intentional breaths.
Allow your breath shift your focus.

ORIENT ☐
Name three things you see _or_ three sensations you feel.
Allow your focus be specific.

GROUND ☐
Breathe intentionally, expanding your belly. Encourage your
exhales to be slightly longer than your inhales. Continue for 8
breaths. When you complete:
Allow your focus be on the feel of your body.

STEP ☐
Name one small adjustment that would support you right now.

_____

Body Check-In

Where do you feel tension?

_____

Where do you feel ease or neutrality?

_____

Field Note

Today I noticed...

_____

Preparation Note

If birth were happening today, what would help me most?

_____

Day _____   **Date** _____

Today's Intention
circle one — or leave blank

Ground   Soothe   Rest   Focus   Release   Curiosity   Excitement

POGS Practice

PAUSE ☐
Take three intentional breaths.
Allow your breath shift your focus.

ORIENT ☐
Name three things you see _or_ three sensations you feel.
Allow your focus be specific.

GROUND ☐
Breathe intentionally, expanding your belly. Encourage your exhales to be slightly longer than your inhales. Continue for 8 breaths. When you complete:
Allow your focus be on the feel of your body.

STEP ☐
Name one small adjustment that would support you right now.

Body Check-In

Where do you feel tension?

Where do you feel ease or neutrality?

Field Note

Today I noticed...

Preparation Note

If birth were happening today, what would help me most?

Day _____   **Date** _____

Today's Intention
circle one — or leave blank

Ground   Soothe   Rest   Focus   Release   Curiosity   Excitement

POGS Practice

PAUSE ☐
Take three intentional breaths.
Allow your breath shift your focus.

ORIENT ☐
Name three things you see _or_ three sensations you feel.
Allow your focus be specific.

GROUND ☐
Breathe intentionally, expanding your belly. Encourage your exhales to be slightly longer than your inhales. Continue for 8 breaths. When you complete:
Allow your focus be on the feel of your body.

STEP ☐
Name one small adjustment that would support you right now.

Body Check-In

Where do you feel tension?

Where do you feel ease or neutrality?

Field Note

Today I noticed...

Preparation Note

If birth were happening today, what would help me most?

Day _____   **Date** _____

Today's Intention
circle one — or leave blank

Ground   Soothe   Rest   Focus   Release   Curiosity   Excitement

POGS Practice

PAUSE ☐
Take three intentional breaths.
Allow your breath shift your focus.

ORIENT ☐
Name three things you see _or_ three sensations you feel.
Allow your focus be specific.

GROUND ☐
Breathe intentionally, expanding your belly. Encourage your
exhales to be slightly longer than your inhales. Continue for 8
breaths. When you complete:
Allow your focus be on the feel of your body.

STEP ☐
Name one small adjustment that would support you right now.

_____

Body Check-In

Where do you feel tension?

_____

Where do you feel ease or neutrality?

_____

Field Note

Today I noticed...

_____

Preparation Note

If birth were happening today, what would help me most?

_____

Day _____   **Date** _____

Today's Intention
circle one — or leave blank

Ground Soothe Rest Focus Release Curiosity Excitement

POGS Practice
PAUSE ☐
Take three intentional breaths.
Allow your breath shift your focus.

ORIENT ☐
Name three things you see _or_ three sensations you feel.
Allow your focus be specific.

GROUND ☐
Breathe intentionally, expanding your belly. Encourage your exhales to be slightly longer than your inhales. Continue for 8 breaths. When you complete:
Allow your focus be on the feel of your body.

STEP ☐
Name one small adjustment that would support you right now.

_____

Body Check-In

Where do you feel tension?

_____

Where do you feel ease or neutrality?

_____

Field Note
Today I noticed...

_____

Preparation Note
If birth were happening today, what would help me most?

_____

Let your breath
be enough
to quiet the noise.

Day _____   Date _____

Today's Intention
circle one — or leave blank

Ground   Soothe   Rest   Focus   Release   Curiosity   Excitement

POGS Practice
PAUSE ☐
Take three intentional breaths.
Allow your breath shift your focus.

ORIENT ☐
Name three things you see *or* three sensations you feel.
Allow your focus be specific.

GROUND ☐
Breathe intentionally, expanding your belly. Encourage your exhales to be slightly longer than your inhales. Continue for 8 breaths. When you complete:
Allow your focus be on the feel of your body.

STEP ☐
Name one small adjustment that would support you right now.

_____

Body Check-In
Where do you feel tension?

_____

Where do you feel ease or neutrality?

_____

Field Note
Today I noticed...

_____

Preparation Note
If birth were happening today, what would help me most?

_____

Day _____   **Date** _____

Today's Intention
circle one — or leave blank

Ground   Soothe   Rest   Focus   Release   Curiosity   Excitement

POGS Practice

PAUSE □
Take three intentional breaths.
Allow your breath shift your focus.

ORIENT □
Name three things you see *or* three sensations you feel.
Allow your focus be specific.

GROUND □
Breathe intentionally, expanding your belly. Encourage your
exhales to be slightly longer than your inhales. Continue for 8
breaths. When you complete:
Allow your focus be on the feel of your body.

STEP □
Name one small adjustment that would support you right now.

_____

Body Check-In

Where do you feel tension?

_____

Where do you feel ease or neutrality?

_____

Field Note

Today I noticed...

_____

Preparation Note

If birth were happening today, what would help me most?

_____

Day

Date

Today's Intention
circle one — or leave blank

Ground   Soothe   Rest   Focus   Release   Curiosity   Excitement

POGS Practice

PAUSE ☐
Take three intentional breaths.
Allow your breath shift your focus.

ORIENT ☐
Name three things you see *or* three sensations you feel.
Allow your focus be specific.

GROUND ☐
Breathe intentionally, expanding your belly. Encourage your
exhales to be slightly longer than your inhales. Continue for 8
breaths. When you complete:
Allow your focus be on the feel of your body.

STEP ☐
Name one small adjustment that would support you right now.

Body Check-In

Where do you feel tension?

Where do you feel ease or neutrality?

Field Note

Today I noticed...

Preparation Note

If birth were happening today, what would help me most?

Day _____   # Date _____

Today's Intention
circle one – or leave blank

Ground   Soothe   Rest   Focus   Release   Curiosity   Excitement

POGS Practice

PAUSE ☐
Take three intentional breaths.
Allow your breath shift your focus.

ORIENT ☐
Name three things you see or three sensations you feel.
Allow your focus be specific.

GROUND ☐
Breathe intentionally, expanding your belly. Encourage your
exhales to be slightly longer than your inhales. Continue for 8
breaths. When you complete:
Allow your focus be on the feel of your body.

STEP ☐
Name one small adjustment that would support you right now.

Body Check-In

Where do you feel tension?

Where do you feel ease or neutrality?

Field Note

Today I noticed...

Preparation Note

If birth were happening today, what would help me most?

Day _____   **Date** _____

Today's Intention
circle one — or leave blank

Ground Soothe Rest Focus Release Curiosity Excitement

POGS Practice

PAUSE □
Take three intentional breaths.
Allow your breath shift your focus.

ORIENT □
Name three things you see *or* three sensations you feel.
Allow your focus be specific.

GROUND □
Breathe intentionally, expanding your belly. Encourage your
exhales to be slightly longer than your inhales. Continue for 8
breaths. When you complete:
Allow your focus be on the feel of your body.

STEP □
Name one small adjustment that would support you right now.

_____

Body Check-In

Where do you feel tension?

_____

Where do you feel ease or neutrality?

_____

Field Note

Today I noticed...

_____

Preparation Note

If birth were happening today, what would help me most?

_____

Day _____   **Date** _____

Today's Intention
circle one — or leave blank

Ground   Soothe   Rest   Focus   Release   Curiosity   Excitement

POGS Practice

PAUSE ☐
Take three intentional breaths.
Allow your breath shift your focus.

ORIENT ☐
Name three things you see *or* three sensations you feel.
Allow your focus be specific.

GROUND ☐
Breathe intentionally, expanding your belly. Encourage your exhales to be slightly longer than your inhales. Continue for 8 breaths. When you complete:
Allow your focus be on the feel of your body.

STEP ☐
Name one small adjustment that would support you right now.

_____

Body Check-In

Where do you feel tension?

_____

Where do you feel ease or neutrality?

_____

Field Note

Today I noticed...

_____

Preparation Note

If birth were happening today, what would help me most?

_____

Day _____   **Date** _____

Today's Intention
circle one — or leave blank

Ground   Soothe   Rest   Focus   Release   Curiosity   Excitement

POGS Practice

PAUSE ☐
Take three intentional breaths.
Allow your breath shift your focus.

ORIENT ☐
Name three things you see *or* three sensations you feel.
Allow your focus be specific.

GROUND ☐
Breathe intentionally, expanding your belly. Encourage your
exhales to be slightly longer than your inhales. Continue for 8
breaths. When you complete:
Allow your focus be on the feel of your body.

STEP ☐
Name one small adjustment that would support you right now.

Body Check-In

Where do you feel tension?

Where do you feel ease or neutrality?

Field Note

Today I noticed...

Preparation Note

If birth were happening today, what would help me most?

Plant your feet.
Let the rest come later.

Day _____   **Date** _____

Today's Intention
circle one — or leave blank

Ground   Soothe   Rest   Focus   Release   Curiosity   Excitement

POGS Practice
PAUSE ☐
Take three intentional breaths.
Allow your breath shift your focus.

ORIENT ☐
Name three things you see *or* three sensations you feel.
Allow your focus be specific.

GROUND ☐
Breathe intentionally, expanding your belly. Encourage your
exhales to be slightly longer than your inhales. Continue for 8
breaths. When you complete:
Allow your focus be on the feel of your body.

STEP ☐
Name one small adjustment that would support you right now.

Body Check-In

Where do you feel tension?

Where do you feel ease or neutrality?

Field Note

Today I noticed...

Preparation Note

If birth were happening today, what would help me most?

Day _____   **Date** _____

Today's Intention
circle one — or leave blank

Ground   Soothe   Rest   Focus   Release   Curiosity   Excitement

POGS Practice

PAUSE ☐
Take three intentional breaths.
Allow your breath shift your focus.

ORIENT ☐
Name three things you see or three sensations you feel.
Allow your focus be specific.

GROUND ☐
Breathe intentionally, expanding your belly. Encourage your exhales to be slightly longer than your inhales. Continue for 8 breaths. When you complete:
Allow your focus be on the feel of your body.

STEP ☐
Name one small adjustment that would support you right now.

_____

Body Check-In

Where do you feel tension?

_____

Where do you feel ease or neutrality?

_____

Field Note

Today I noticed...

_____

Preparation Note

If birth were happening today, what would help me most?

_____

Day _____   **Date** _____

Today's Intention
circle one — or leave blank

Ground Soothe Rest Focus Release Curiosity Excitement

POGS Practice

PAUSE ☐
Take three intentional breaths.
Allow your breath shift your focus.

ORIENT ☐
Name three things you see or three sensations you feel.
Allow your focus be specific.

GROUND ☐
Breathe intentionally, expanding your belly. Encourage your
exhales to be slightly longer than your inhales. Continue for 8
breaths. When you complete:
Allow your focus be on the feel of your body.

STEP ☐
Name one small adjustment that would support you right now.

_____

Body Check-In

Where do you feel tension?

_____

Where do you feel ease or neutrality?

_____

Field Note

Today I noticed...

_____

Preparation Note

If birth were happening today, what would help me most?

_____

Day _____   **Date** _____

Today's Intention
circle one — or leave blank

Ground   Soothe   Rest   Focus   Release   Curiosity   Excitement

POGS Practice

PAUSE ☐
Take three intentional breaths.
Allow your breath shift your focus.

ORIENT ☐
Name three things you see _or_ three sensations you feel.
Allow your focus be specific.

GROUND ☐
Breathe intentionally, expanding your belly. Encourage your
exhales to be slightly longer than your inhales. Continue for 8
breaths. When you complete:
Allow your focus be on the feel of your body.

STEP ☐
Name one small adjustment that would support you right now.

Body Check-In

Where do you feel tension?

Where do you feel ease or neutrality?

Field Note

Today I noticed...

Preparation Note

If birth were happening today, what would help me most?

Day _____   **Date** _____

Today's Intention
circle one — or leave blank

Ground   Soothe   Rest   Focus   Release   Curiosity   Excitement

POGS Practice

PAUSE ☐
Take three intentional breaths.
Allow your breath shift your focus.

ORIENT ☐
Name three things you see _or_ three sensations you feel.
Allow your focus be specific.

GROUND ☐
Breathe intentionally, expanding your belly. Encourage your exhales to be slightly longer than your inhales. Continue for 8 breaths. When you complete:
Allow your focus be on the feel of your body.

STEP ☐
Name one small adjustment that would support you right now.

Body Check-In

Where do you feel tension?

Where do you feel ease or neutrality?

Field Note

Today I noticed...

Preparation Note

If birth were happening today, what would help me most?

Day _____   **Date** _____

Today's Intention
circle one — or leave blank

Ground   Soothe   Rest   Focus   Release   Curiosity   Excitement

POGS Practice

PAUSE ☐
Take three intentional breaths.
Allow your breath shift your focus.

ORIENT ☐
Name three things you see *or* three sensations you feel.
Allow your focus be specific.

GROUND ☐
Breathe intentionally, expanding your belly. Encourage your exhales to be slightly longer than your inhales. Continue for 8 breaths. When you complete:
Allow your focus be on the feel of your body.

STEP ☐
Name one small adjustment that would support you right now.

Body Check-In

Where do you feel tension?

Where do you feel ease or neutrality?

Field Note

Today I noticed...

Preparation Note

If birth were happening today, what would help me most?

Day

Date

Today's Intention
circle one — or leave blank

Ground   Soothe   Rest   Focus   Release   Curiosity   Excitement

POGS Practice

PAUSE ☐
Take three intentional breaths.
Allow your breath shift your focus.

ORIENT ☐
Name three things you see *or* three sensations you feel.
Allow your focus be specific.

GROUND ☐
Breathe intentionally, expanding your belly. Encourage your
exhales to be slightly longer than your inhales. Continue for 8
breaths. When you complete:
Allow your focus be on the feel of your body.

STEP ☐
Name one small adjustment that would support you right now.

Body Check-In

Where do you feel tension?

Where do you feel ease or neutrality?

Field Note

Today I noticed...

Preparation Note

If birth were happening today, what would help me most?

Take Up Space

Day _____   **Date** _____

Today's Intention
circle one — or leave blank

Ground   Soothe   Rest   Focus   Release   Curiosity   Excitement

POGS Practice

PAUSE ☐
Take three intentional breaths.
Allow your breath shift your focus.

ORIENT ☐
Name three things you see _or_ three sensations you feel.
Allow your focus be specific.

GROUND ☐
Breathe intentionally, expanding your belly. Encourage your exhales to be slightly longer than your inhales. Continue for 8 breaths. When you complete:
Allow your focus be on the feel of your body.

STEP ☐
Name one small adjustment that would support you right now.

Body Check-In

Where do you feel tension?

Where do you feel ease or neutrality?

Field Note

Today I noticed...

Preparation Note

If birth were happening today, what would help me most?

Day _____   **Date** _____

Today's Intention
circle one — or leave blank

Ground Soothe Rest Focus Release Curiosity Excitement

POGS Practice

PAUSE □
Take three intentional breaths.
Allow your breath shift your focus.

ORIENT □
Name three things you see _or_ three sensations you feel.
Allow your focus be specific.

GROUND □
Breathe intentionally, expanding your belly. Encourage your
exhales to be slightly longer than your inhales. Continue for 8
breaths. When you complete:
Allow your focus be on the feel of your body.

STEP □
Name one small adjustment that would support you right now.

_____

Body Check-In

Where do you feel tension?

_____

Where do you feel ease or neutrality?

_____

Field Note

Today I noticed...

_____

Preparation Note

If birth were happening today, what would help me most?

_____

Day

Date

Today's Intention
circle one — or leave blank

Ground Soothe Rest Focus Release Curiosity Excitement

POGS Practice
PAUSE □
Take three intentional breaths.
Allow your breath shift your focus.

ORIENT □
Name three things you see *or* three sensations you feel.
Allow your focus be specific.

GROUND □
Breathe intentionally, expanding your belly. Encourage your
exhales to be slightly longer than your inhales. Continue for 8
breaths. When you complete:
Allow your focus be on the feel of your body.

STEP □
Name one small adjustment that would support you right now.

Body Check-In

Where do you feel tension?

Where do you feel ease or neutrality?

Field Note
Today I noticed...

Preparation Note
If birth were happening today, what would help me most?

Day _____   **Date** _____

Today's Intention
circle one — or leave blank

Ground   Soothe   Rest   Focus   Release   Curiosity   Excitement

POGS Practice

PAUSE ☐
Take three intentional breaths.
Allow your breath shift your focus.

ORIENT ☐
Name three things you see _or_ three sensations you feel.
Allow your focus be specific.

GROUND ☐
Breathe intentionally, expanding your belly. Encourage your exhales to be slightly longer than your inhales. Continue for 8 breaths. When you complete:
Allow your focus be on the feel of your body.

STEP ☐
Name one small adjustment that would support you right now.

_____

Body Check-In

Where do you feel tension?

_____

Where do you feel ease or neutrality?

_____

Field Note

Today I noticed...

_____

Preparation Note

If birth were happening today, what would help me most?

_____

Day

Date

Today's Intention
circle one — or leave blank

Ground   Soothe   Rest   Focus   Release   Curiosity   Excitement

POGS Practice

PAUSE ☐
Take three intentional breaths.
Allow your breath shift your focus.

ORIENT ☐
Name three things you see *or* three sensations you feel.
Allow your focus be specific.

GROUND ☐
Breathe intentionally, expanding your belly. Encourage your
exhales to be slightly longer than your inhales. Continue for 8
breaths. When you complete:
Allow your focus be on the feel of your body.

STEP ☐
Name one small adjustment that would support you right now.

Body Check-In

Where do you feel tension?

Where do you feel ease or neutrality?

Field Note

Today I noticed...

Preparation Note

If birth were happening today, what would help me most?

Day _____   **Date** _____

Today's Intention
circle one – or leave blank

Ground   Soothe   Rest   Focus   Release   Curiosity   Excitement

POGS Practice
PAUSE ☐
Take three intentional breaths.
Allow your breath shift your focus.

ORIENT ☐
Name three things you see _or_ three sensations you feel.
Allow your focus be specific.

GROUND ☐
Breathe intentionally, expanding your belly. Encourage your
exhales to be slightly longer than your inhales. Continue for 8
breaths. When you complete:
Allow your focus be on the feel of your body.

STEP ☐
Name one small adjustment that would support you right now.

_____

Body Check-In

Where do you feel tension?

_____

Where do you feel ease or neutrality?

_____

Field Note

Today I noticed...

_____

Preparation Note

If birth were happening today, what would help me most?

_____

Day _____   **Date** _____

Today's Intention
circle one — or leave blank

Ground Soothe Rest Focus Release Curiosity Excitement

POGS Practice

PAUSE ☐
Take three intentional breaths.
Allow your breath shift your focus.

ORIENT ☐
Name three things you see or three sensations you feel.
Allow your focus be specific.

GROUND ☐
Breathe intentionally, expanding your belly. Encourage your
exhales to be slightly longer than your inhales. Continue for 8
breaths. When you complete:
Allow your focus be on the feel of your body.

STEP ☐
Name one small adjustment that would support you right now.

Body Check-In

Where do you feel tension?

Where do you feel ease or neutrality?

Field Note

Today I noticed...

Preparation Note

If birth were happening today, what would help me most?

Let Your Breath
Guide You

Day _____   **Date** _____

Today's Intention
circle one — or leave blank

Ground Soothe Rest Focus Release Curiosity Excitement

POGS Practice

PAUSE ☐
Take three intentional breaths.
Allow your breath shift your focus.

ORIENT ☐
Name three things you see _or_ three sensations you feel.
Allow your focus be specific.

GROUND ☐
Breathe intentionally, expanding your belly. Encourage your
exhales to be slightly longer than your inhales. Continue for 8
breaths. When you complete:
Allow your focus be on the feel of your body.

STEP ☐
Name one small adjustment that would support you right now.

_____

Body Check-In

Where do you feel tension?

_____

Where do you feel ease or neutrality?

_____

Field Note

Today I noticed...

_____

Preparation Note

If birth were happening today, what would help me most?

_____

Day _____   **Date** _____

Today's Intention
circle one — or leave blank

Ground Soothe Rest Focus Release Curiosity Excitement

POGS Practice

PAUSE ☐
Take three intentional breaths.
Allow your breath shift your focus.

ORIENT ☐
Name three things you see _or_ three sensations you feel.
Allow your focus be specific.

GROUND ☐
Breathe intentionally, expanding your belly. Encourage your
exhales to be slightly longer than your inhales. Continue for 8
breaths. When you complete:
Allow your focus be on the feel of your body.

STEP ☐
Name one small adjustment that would support you right now.

_____

Body Check-In

Where do you feel tension?

_____

Where do you feel ease or neutrality?

_____

Field Note

Today I noticed...

_____

Preparation Note

If birth were happening today, what would help me most?

_____

Day   # Date

Today's Intention
circle one — or leave blank

Ground Soothe Rest Focus Release Curiosity Excitement

POGS Practice

PAUSE □
Take three intentional breaths.
Allow your breath shift your focus.

ORIENT □
Name three things you see *or* three sensations you feel.
Allow your focus be specific.

GROUND □
Breathe intentionally, expanding your belly. Encourage your
exhales to be slightly longer than your inhales. Continue for 8
breaths. When you complete:
Allow your focus be on the feel of your body.

STEP □
Name one small adjustment that would support you right now.

Body Check-In

Where do you feel tension?

Where do you feel ease or neutrality?

Field Note

Today I noticed...

Preparation Note

If birth were happening today, what would help me most?

Day

Date

Today's Intention
circle one – or leave blank

Ground   Soothe   Rest   Focus   Release   Curiosity   Excitement

POGS Practice

PAUSE ☐
Take three intentional breaths.
Allow your breath shift your focus.

ORIENT ☐
Name three things you see *or* three sensations you feel.
Allow your focus be specific.

GROUND ☐
Breathe intentionally, expanding your belly. Encourage your
exhales to be slightly longer than your inhales. Continue for 8
breaths. When you complete:
Allow your focus be on the feel of your body.

STEP ☐
Name one small adjustment that would support you right now.

Body Check-In

Where do you feel tension?

Where do you feel ease or neutrality?

Field Note

Today I noticed...

Preparation Note

If birth were happening today, what would help me most?

Day _____   **Date** _____

Today's Intention
circle one — or leave blank

Ground Soothe Rest Focus Release Curiosity Excitement

POGS Practice

PAUSE □
Take three intentional breaths.
Allow your breath shift your focus.

ORIENT □
Name three things you see or three sensations you feel.
Allow your focus be specific.

GROUND □
Breathe intentionally, expanding your belly. Encourage your
exhales to be slightly longer than your inhales. Continue for 8
breaths. When you complete:
Allow your focus be on the feel of your body.

STEP □
Name one small adjustment that would support you right now.

_____

Body Check-In

Where do you feel tension?

_____

Where do you feel ease or neutrality?

_____

Field Note

Today I noticed...

_____

Preparation Note

If birth were happening today, what would help me most?

_____

Day _____   **Date** _____

Today's Intention
circle one — or leave blank

Ground   Soothe   Rest   Focus   Release   Curiosity   Excitement

POGS Practice
PAUSE ☐
Take three intentional breaths.
Allow your breath shift your focus.

ORIENT ☐
Name three things you see _or_ three sensations you feel.
Allow your focus be specific.

GROUND ☐
Breathe intentionally, expanding your belly. Encourage your
exhales to be slightly longer than your inhales. Continue for 8
breaths. When you complete:
Allow your focus be on the feel of your body.

STEP ☐
Name one small adjustment that would support you right now.

Body Check-In

Where do you feel tension?

Where do you feel ease or neutrality?

Field Note

Today I noticed...

Preparation Note

If birth were happening today, what would help me most?

Day _____   **Date** _____

Today's Intention
circle one — or leave blank

Ground   Soothe   Rest   Focus   Release   Curiosity   Excitement

POGS Practice
PAUSE ☐
Take three intentional breaths.
Allow your breath shift your focus.

ORIENT ☐
Name three things you see _or_ three sensations you feel.
Allow your focus be specific.

GROUND ☐
Breathe intentionally, expanding your belly. Encourage your
exhales to be slightly longer than your inhales. Continue for 8
breaths. When you complete:
Allow your focus be on the feel of your body.

STEP ☐
Name one small adjustment that would support you right now.

Body Check-In

Where do you feel tension?

Where do you feel ease or neutrality?

Field Note

Today I noticed...

Preparation Note

If birth were happening today, what would help me most?

Notice how far you've already come.

Day _____   **Date** _____

Today's Intention
circle one — or leave blank

Ground   Soothe   Rest   Focus   Release   Curiosity   Excitement

POGS Practice
PAUSE ☐
Take three intentional breaths.
Allow your breath shift your focus.

ORIENT ☐
Name three things you see *or* three sensations you feel.
Allow your focus be specific.

GROUND ☐
Breathe intentionally, expanding your belly. Encourage your
exhales to be slightly longer than your inhales. Continue for 8
breaths. When you complete:
Allow your focus be on the feel of your body.

STEP ☐
Name one small adjustment that would support you right now.

Body Check-In

Where do you feel tension?

Where do you feel ease or neutrality?

Field Note
Today I noticed...

Preparation Note
If birth were happening today, what would help me most?

Day _____   **Date** _____

Today's Intention
circle one – or leave blank

Ground   Soothe   Rest   Focus   Release   Curiosity   Excitement

POGS Practice

PAUSE ☐
Take three intentional breaths.
Allow your breath shift your focus.

ORIENT ☐
Name three things you see or three sensations you feel.
Allow your focus be specific.

GROUND ☐
Breathe intentionally, expanding your belly. Encourage your exhales to be slightly longer than your inhales. Continue for 8 breaths. When you complete:
Allow your focus be on the feel of your body.

STEP ☐
Name one small adjustment that would support you right now.

_____

Body Check-In

Where do you feel tension?

_____

Where do you feel ease or neutrality?

_____

Field Note

Today I noticed...

_____

Preparation Note

If birth were happening today, what would help me most?

_____

Day _____   **Date** _____

Today's Intention
circle one — or leave blank

Ground   Soothe   Rest   Focus   Release   Curiosity   Excitement

POGS Practice

PAUSE ☐
Take three intentional breaths.
Allow your breath shift your focus.

ORIENT ☐
Name three things you see or three sensations you feel.
Allow your focus be specific.

GROUND ☐
Breathe intentionally, expanding your belly. Encourage your exhales to be slightly longer than your inhales. Continue for 8 breaths. When you complete:
Allow your focus be on the feel of your body.

STEP ☐
Name one small adjustment that would support you right now.

Body Check-In

Where do you feel tension?

Where do you feel ease or neutrality?

Field Note

Today I noticed...

Preparation Note

If birth were happening today, what would help me most?

Day _____   **Date**

Today's Intention
circle one — or leave blank

Ground   Soothe   Rest   Focus   Release   Curiosity   Excitement

POGS Practice

PAUSE ☐
Take three intentional breaths.
Allow your breath shift your focus.

ORIENT ☐
Name three things you see _or_ three sensations you feel.
Allow your focus be specific.

GROUND ☐
Breathe intentionally, expanding your belly. Encourage your exhales to be slightly longer than your inhales. Continue for 8 breaths. When you complete:
Allow your focus be on the feel of your body.

STEP ☐
Name one small adjustment that would support you right now.

Body Check-In

Where do you feel tension?

Where do you feel ease or neutrality?

Field Note

Today I noticed...

Preparation Note

If birth were happening today, what would help me most?

Day   Date

Today's Intention
circle one – or leave blank

Ground Soothe Rest Focus Release Curiosity Excitement

POGS Practice
PAUSE ☐
Take three intentional breaths.
Allow your breath shift your focus.

ORIENT ☐
Name three things you see *or* three sensations you feel.
Allow your focus be specific.

GROUND ☐
Breathe intentionally, expanding your belly. Encourage your
exhales to be slightly longer than your inhales. Continue for 8
breaths. When you complete:
Allow your focus be on the feel of your body.

STEP ☐
Name one small adjustment that would support you right now.

Body Check-In

Where do you feel tension?

Where do you feel ease or neutrality?

Field Note

Today I noticed...

Preparation Note

If birth were happening today, what would help me most?

Day _____ **Date** _____

Today's Intention
circle one — or leave blank

Ground   Soothe   Rest   Focus   Release   Curiosity   Excitement

POGS Practice

PAUSE ☐
Take three intentional breaths.
Allow your breath shift your focus.

ORIENT ☐
Name three things you see *or* three sensations you feel.
Allow your focus be specific.

GROUND ☐
Breathe intentionally, expanding your belly. Encourage your
exhales to be slightly longer than your inhales. Continue for 8
breaths. When you complete:
Allow your focus be on the feel of your body.

STEP ☐
Name one small adjustment that would support you right now.

_____

Body Check-In

Where do you feel tension?

_____

Where do you feel ease or neutrality?

_____

Field Note

Today I noticed...

_____

Preparation Note

If birth were happening today, what would help me most?

_____

Day _____   **Date** _____

Today's Intention
circle one — or leave blank

Ground Soothe Rest Focus Release Curiosity Excitement

POGS Practice

PAUSE ☐
Take three intentional breaths.
Allow your breath shift your focus.

ORIENT ☐
Name three things you see _or_ three sensations you feel.
Allow your focus be specific.

GROUND ☐
Breathe intentionally, expanding your belly. Encourage your
exhales to be slightly longer than your inhales. Continue for 8
breaths. When you complete:
Allow your focus be on the feel of your body.

STEP ☐
Name one small adjustment that would support you right now.

Body Check-In

Where do you feel tension?

Where do you feel ease or neutrality?

Field Note

Today I noticed...

Preparation Note

If birth were happening today, what would help me most?

Trust
What
You
Notice

Day _____   **Date** _____

Today's Intention
circle one — or leave blank

Ground   Soothe   Rest   Focus   Release   Curiosity   Excitement

POGS Practice

PAUSE ☐
Take three intentional breaths.
Allow your breath shift your focus.

ORIENT ☐
Name three things you see _or_ three sensations you feel.
Allow your focus be specific.

GROUND ☐
Breathe intentionally, expanding your belly. Encourage your
exhales to be slightly longer than your inhales. Continue for 8
breaths. When you complete:
Allow your focus be on the feel of your body.

STEP ☐
Name one small adjustment that would support you right now.

_____

Body Check-In

Where do you feel tension?

_____

Where do you feel ease or neutrality?

_____

Field Note

Today I noticed...

_____

Preparation Note

If birth were happening today, what would help me most?

_____

Day _____   **Date** _____

Today's Intention
circle one — or leave blank

Ground   Soothe   Rest   Focus   Release   Curiosity   Excitement

POGS Practice

PAUSE ☐
Take three intentional breaths.
Allow your breath shift your focus.

ORIENT ☐
Name three things you see *or* three sensations you feel.
Allow your focus be specific.

GROUND ☐
Breathe intentionally, expanding your belly. Encourage your
exhales to be slightly longer than your inhales. Continue for 8
breaths. When you complete:
Allow your focus be on the feel of your body.

STEP ☐
Name one small adjustment that would support you right now.

_____

Body Check-In

Where do you feel tension?

_____

Where do you feel ease or neutrality?

_____

Field Note

Today I noticed...

_____

Preparation Note

If birth were happening today, what would help me most?

_____

Day _____   **Date** _____

Today's Intention
circle one — or leave blank

Ground Soothe Rest Focus Release Curiosity Excitement

POGS Practice
PAUSE ☐
Take three intentional breaths.
Allow your breath shift your focus.

ORIENT ☐
Name three things you see _or_ three sensations you feel.
Allow your focus be specific.

GROUND ☐
Breathe intentionally, expanding your belly. Encourage your exhales to be slightly longer than your inhales. Continue for 8 breaths. When you complete:
Allow your focus be on the feel of your body.

STEP ☐
Name one small adjustment that would support you right now.

_____

Body Check-In
Where do you feel tension?

_____

Where do you feel ease or neutrality?

_____

Field Note
Today I noticed...

_____

Preparation Note
If birth were happening today, what would help me most?

_____

Day _____   **Date** _____

Today's Intention
circle one — or leave blank

Ground   Soothe   Rest   Focus   Release   Curiosity   Excitement

POGS Practice

PAUSE ☐
Take three intentional breaths.
Allow your breath shift your focus.

ORIENT ☐
Name three things you see _or_ three sensations you feel.
Allow your focus be specific.

GROUND ☐
Breathe intentionally, expanding your belly. Encourage your
exhales to be slightly longer than your inhales. Continue for 8
breaths. When you complete:
Allow your focus be on the feel of your body.

STEP ☐
Name one small adjustment that would support you right now.

Body Check-In

Where do you feel tension?

Where do you feel ease or neutrality?

Field Note

Today I noticed...

Preparation Note

If birth were happening today, what would help me most?

Day   **Date**

Today's Intention
circle one — or leave blank

Ground Soothe Rest Focus Release Curiosity Excitement

POGS Practice

PAUSE □
Take three intentional breaths.
Allow your breath shift your focus.

ORIENT □
Name three things you see *or* three sensations you feel.
Allow your focus be specific.

GROUND □
Breathe intentionally, expanding your belly. Encourage your exhales to be slightly longer than your inhales. Continue for 8 breaths. When you complete:
Allow your focus be on the feel of your body.

STEP □
Name one small adjustment that would support you right now.

Body Check-In

Where do you feel tension?

Where do you feel ease or neutrality?

Field Note

Today I noticed...

Preparation Note

If birth were happening today, what would help me most?

Day _____   **Date** _____

Today's Intention
circle one — or leave blank

Ground   Soothe   Rest   Focus   Release   Curiosity   Excitement

POGS Practice

PAUSE □
Take three intentional breaths.
Allow your breath shift your focus.

ORIENT □
Name three things you see *or* three sensations you feel.
Allow your focus be specific.

GROUND □
Breathe intentionally, expanding your belly. Encourage your
exhales to be slightly longer than your inhales. Continue for 8
breaths. When you complete:
Allow your focus be on the feel of your body.

STEP □
Name one small adjustment that would support you right now.

Body Check-In

Where do you feel tension?

Where do you feel ease or neutrality?

Field Note

Today I noticed...

Preparation Note

If birth were happening today, what would help me most?

Hello Again,

Have you been enjoying your journey?
What did you discover?

I hope your reflections brought insight or awareness.
Remember: practice makes prepared, not perfect.

Birth doesn't need to be perfect — or even easy — for you to be able to navigate it.

You already know how to orient.
You already know how to pause, notice, ground, and take the next step.

If there is more of your journey to track, begin again.
If birth is approaching, take a moment to look back at what you've already done.

Each day has been a step forward.
Orientation comes from inside you, and through this process, you've learned the way.
You can navigate even the toughest peaks.

I believe in you,
Dr. V